Your First Triathlon

A Beginners Guide To Triathlon Training, Triathlon Preparation And Completing Your First Triathlon

Richard Bond

Copyright © HRD Publishing 2015

All rights reserved.

ISBN-13: 978-1512268713
ISBN-10: 1512268712

CONTENTS

1	Introduction	6
2	Chapter 1. An Introduction to Triathlon	7
3	Chapter 2. The Swim	13
4	Chapter 3. The Bike	27
5	Chapter 4. The Run	58
6	Chapter 5. Your Very Own Triathlon Training Plans	71
7	Chapter 6. Nutrition and Hydration Basics	85
8	Chapter 7. Race Day	89
9	Conclusion	93
	About The Author	94
	Other Books By Richard Bond	96

INTRODUCTION

Completing your first triathlon is a daunting task. There are so many things to think about before you even start such as, what race to enter, which training program should you follow, should you eat differently, what equipment or technology can help, are you physically and mentally strong enough to complete it and the list goes on. This book will help you answer all of these questions and alleviate some of the fear attached to completing a triathlon for the first time.

What are you going to learn?

I'm going to help you select the appropriate race distance for your needs. I'm going to show you how to train depending on your goals. I'll show you how to improve in all areas of the triathlon from Swimming, Cycling, Running and the Transitions. I'm going to teach you the mindset to have to be successful. I'll show you the equipment and gadgets that can help you cross the finish line. I'll teach you the basics on nutrition and hydration. I'll show you how to prepare for a race. I'll teach you how to avoid mistakes and share the top tips that helped me cross the line for the first time.

This book is designed to help the first time Triathlete cross the finish line in a simple and effective way.

Are you ready to take on one of the biggest challenges of your life?

CHAPTER 1. AN INTRODUCTION TO TRIATHLON

To the uninitiated, the sport of triathlon can be a very confusing endeavor. Consider: just to finish one race, you'd have to complete a swim, then hop on to your bike for a ride, before finishing up with a run. Any one of those events is already taxing enough by itself. Stringing them together to make up one race is borderline insane. When you throw in the concept of a full distance triathlon race (Also known as the Ironman Triathlon) consisting of a 3.8 kilometer swim, a 180 kilometer bike ride, and topped off by a 42.2 kilometer full marathon, then things can quickly devolve into something else beyond crazy or insane.

And yet, triathlon nowadays is one of the world's fastest growing sports. Athletes and amateurs from all sorts of background inevitably find themselves embracing all three disciplines to become a full-fledged triathlete. Many who only used to swim before eventually made it to triathlon. You can say the same for cyclists turned triathletes or runners who decided to expand their repertoire by learning to bike and swim as well.

So, what is in triathlon that makes it a crowd favorite? Is it the prestige that has come to define triathlon over the last few years? Is it the challenge? If it is such a difficult sport (or combination of sports) then why is it growing by the minute? Who in their right mind would want to try and take on three different and unique sporting disciplines, train in all of them, and be proficient in all of them, just to become a triathlete? What is it in triathlon that just begs for people to embrace it?

Well, as it turns out, there are many reasons why triathlon is a fast-growing sport.

What many people consider as the thing that makes triathlon difficult - it's multi-sport approach – is a welcome challenge for many people. Training in just one sport can quickly become boring and monotonous. Try training for a full marathon or an ultra-marathon and the countless hours and miles you spend mostly on your own can begin to take its toll after a while.

Triathlon doesn't suffer from that kind of problem. If you're bored running, swap your running shoes for cycling cleats and you're off. If you're tired of biking, you can always jump on to a pool or train at the local beach. The different facets of triathlon training and racing never result in a dull day. You end up doing so many things that there is simply no room for boredom or monotony.

This, in turn, creates a lot of physical advantages that can help boost any triathlete, amateur or otherwise. The multisport aspect of triathlon helps you become a more holistic athlete. You don't just train your legs as you run or bike, you also train your upper body through the swim. All three disciplines engage your core and that, if nothing else, is one of the better pathways to washboard abs – although many triathletes would be the first to tell you that triathlon training does not necessarily equal a sculpted body, and many are just fine with that.

Aside from a more holistic training approach, triathlon training also helps minimize injury. Because you're not doing the same thing over and over again, day in and day out, you can minimize the likelihood of overloading a specific body part, which is often a cause for injury. Runners, for example, are prone to leg injuries because they use their legs and nothing else. Worse yet, the repetitive exposure to impact forces when you run are concentrated on specific muscles and joints only and are really not distributed across the entire leg, so the overloading becomes much worse on just a few body parts. You can say the same for cyclists or swimmers or any other athlete.

This, among other things, is the beauty of triathlon. It is a difficult sport, yes, but it is also rewarding, challenging, and addicting. Training for a triathlon never leads to a dull day. Perhaps that's why many ultimately want to become a triathlete.

Still, regardless of your reasons, I would like to congratulate you for making the decision to train for your first triathlon. The road ahead is not easy, but like I've said it will be fulfilling and addicting. And it will only make you a much better and more complete athlete.

If you're ready, let's get on with it!

The Current Triathlon Scene

The most popular word that is associated with triathlon racing is "Ironman", and the phrase "I want to be an Ironman" is very common among triathlon circles. But that's just one aspect of the sport. The term "Ironman" is basically a brand name and is copyrighted to the World Triathlon Corporation (WTC).

There are many other brands that manage different triathlon races all around the world. One up-and-coming competitor to the "Ironman" moniker is the Challenge Family series and one of its most iconic races takes place in a small village in Germany called Roth. The Norseman Triathlon in Norway is also gaining some appeal among hardcore triathlon enthusiasts. Of course, the Ironman brand remains as a major attraction for many athletes who are new to the sport, and there's a big chance you are reading this book right now because a friend introduced you to Ironman triathlon racing or because you've seen it on TV.

In addition to these, there are also national and international organizations that run different triathlon events around the world including the International Triathlon Union and USA Triathlon. Those two organizations who tend to focus on shorter races have defined the following distances as the standard offering for triathlon races around the world:

- **Sprint Distance:** consisting of a 750-meter (0.47-mile) swim, 20-kilometer (12-mile) bike, and a 5-kilometer (3.1-mile) run.

- **Intermediate Distance** (sometimes referred to as the "Standard Distance") also commonly called the "Olympic distance" because this is the format used in the triathlon at the Olympics: consisting of a 1.5-kilometer (0.93-mile) swim, 40-kilometer (25-mile) bike, and 10-kilometer (6.2-mile) run. This race is also sometimes called a 5150 referring to the total cumulative distance in kilometers.

- **Long Course:** consisting of a 1.9-kilometer (1.2-mile) swim, 90-kilometer (56-mile) bike, and a 21.1-kilometer (13.1-mile) run (half marathon). In the Ironman series, this distance is referred to as the 70.3 referring to the total cumulative distance in miles.

- **Ultra Distance** commonly referred to as 140.6 (total distance in miles, equivalent to 226.2 km) or the "Ironman": consisting of a 3.8-kilometer (2.4-mile) swim, 180.2-kilometer (112.0-mile) bike, and a 42.2-kilometer (26.2-mile) run (full marathon).

For purposes of this book, we will focus on training for the sprint distance with some remarks about going up to Olympic distance racing. As you will quickly find out, many of the tips and tricks you will learn from training for a sprint distance race can be quickly scaled up to apply to longer distance races. Naturally, the exact distances in your training will change but other than that, the equipment and strategies remain mostly the same.

Now that you've gotten a basic picture of triathlon, let's go ahead and talk about the finer details of the sport.

What Makes a Triathlon

The name triathlon is almost self-explanatory. The "tri" part represents the "three sport" discipline of triathlon while the Greek "athlon" means contest which refers to the racing aspect of the sport.

While there are other three sport versions of triathlon, the most well-known and the one we'll end up discussing in this book, is the one consisting of swimming, cycling and running, in that specific order.

This brings us to the typical way triathlon races are timed. Any particular triathlon race is broken down into five specific sections:

- The swim time, consisting of the total time you spent from the gun start of the swim up until that moment when you get out of the water.
- T1 (or Transition 1) time, referring to the time in the transition area between the swim leg and the bike leg.
- The cycling time, referring to the total cycling time from the start of the mount up to the dismount line.
- T2 (or Transition 2) time, referring to the time in the transition area between the bike leg and the run leg.

- The run time, referring to the total time you spent on the run leg up to the finish line.

In some cases, the T1 time is often included into the cycling leg and the T2 time included in the run leg.

In completing your first triathlon, you might be inclined to just focus on the goal of completing the race – unless you're the ultra-competitive kind, in which case time might be more of a priority. After this, you can then focus on improving your finishing time in your succeeding races.

The best way to do this is to look at the breakdown for each leg – known commonly as splits – and identify which leg you lost time the most in. From there, you can put more effort into training in the leg that you're weak in and hopefully that translates into a faster overall time.

But enough of looking too far ahead into the future; for now, our primary objective is to get you from where you are currently, to the starting line and into the finish line with the end goal of making the process and journey so enjoyable that you'll be motivated to do more after your first one.

If you're ready, let's go ahead and begin your triathlon journey.

CHAPTER 2. THE SWIM

It inevitably begins with the swim.

Now, let's get one thing clear here: this book will not teach you how to swim. If you're one of those athletes who have yet to begin training for the swim – or worse, you still don't know how to swim – then fear not. When it comes to swimming, you can teach even the oldest dog new tricks.

Learning How to Swim

So, let's cover this topic very quickly just to get it out of the way.

If you don't know how to swim yet, take note of the following tips to get you going on the water as soon as possible:

1. **Get a swim coach or enroll in a swimming class as soon as possible**

    One of the most common reasons why many athletes don't know how to swim is that they are afraid of the water. Consequently, they keep putting off the decision to learn how to swim. That cycle of wanting to and then backing out of the decision to learn to swim just kicks the can down the road and you never end up learning.

    If you are truly serious with becoming a triathlete and swimming is your weakest area, get into a swim school today. There are many organizations that offer swim sessions for various purposes, from the most basic swimming skills to improving your efficiency in the water, and you need to pick the one that suits your needs best. Typically, you'll end up paying for a certain number of sessions to complete the course, and that's best because that will force you to come back for another go on a regular basis.

There's one thing, however, that you need to keep in mind when trying to find a swim coach; it is important that you feel comfortable with your coach especially if you really have zero skills in the water. One major roadblock to learning how to swim is that coach and student don't communicate well. Either the student is too shy to talk to the coach to figure out the areas for improvement, or the coach is too militaristic or even frustrated with having a student that doesn't know how to do anything in the water.

To remedy this, talk to your potential coaches before signing up. Make sure you set very clear expectations. If you really don't know how to swim, be open and honest outright and see how they respond to that information. You want them to have a very clear picture of your current situation and you want them to understand why you want to learn to swim. If you build this foundation properly, you'll have great swimming sessions ahead of you; if you don't, you'll have a ton of headaches trying to learn to swim with a coach that you don't like and is frustrated with you.

2. Schedule your swim session regularly

Don't do once a week swim sessions especially if you don't know anything about swimming. Three times a week sessions are more preferable.

Swimming is such a technical sport that it's easy to forget the things you learned during the first session and carry them over to the second session if those two sessions are a week apart.

Instead, schedule your swim sessions every two days or so if you're still trying to figure out the basic points of swimming.

This will force you to learn quicker and in the process retain more during the shorter intervals between sessions.

3. Don't splurge on gear out right

In the next sessions, we'll talk about a bunch of gear essential to a swimmer who wants to do well on the water. For beginners, however, the basic swim gear will more than suffice.

I don't want to hammer this message more than necessary so get the most basic gear – swim goggles, a swim cap, and swim jammers – and you're already good to go.

And there you have it: you're basic introduction to learning how to swim. Make sure you take care of this section first before coming back to read the rest of the chapter on swim training for a triathlon.

Don't worry, I'll wait. I'll be just right here when you're ready.

Swim Gear

Let's start with your swim gear. Let's assume that you already have the requisite goggles and swim cap as mentioned in the previous section; it's now time to expand your swim toys to include more practical workout aids that can help you become more efficient in the water.

1. **Pull buoys.** A pull buoy is typically made of foam and shaped like a lazily drawn #8. You need pull buoys if you want to work on your upper body strength to improve your "pull." Basically, the equipment is designed to keep your lower body still and still correctly positioned just below the water's surface while your upper body does all the hard work in training.

2. **Kickboards.** You typically see kids at the local pool playing with kickboards as a flotation device. It's designed to do the opposite of what pull buoys do; you rest your hands on kickboards and allow your legs to do the work. It's basically used to practice your kick while keeping your upper body in the right position on the water.

3. **Hand paddles.** These are also used to train your upper body strength by adding resistance to your pull stroke. Basically, you're putting paddles on your hands so you catch more water and pull harder. For beginners, it is advisable to get smaller hand paddles with holes to reduce the resistance and prevent injuries to the elbows and shoulders. As you gain more experience and strength, you can gradually transition to bigger hand paddles to continue building up upper body strength.

4. **Snorkels.** Not everyone uses them but they can be of tremendous benefit if you want to focus on your head position, body position and stroke in the water. Breathing contorts your body enough that inexperienced swimmers tend to lose the position when they breathe; snorkels allow you to remain submerged in the water without having to worry about altering your position to breathe.

5. **Underwater Music Player.** If you're fond of doing long reps at the pool and you'd love to do so while still listening to your favorite song, you might want to consider getting an underwater music player. These devices work a bit differently than your standard music player; instead of going into your ear, the speakers instead connect to your upper cheekbone. The vibrations are still picked up by your earn as music and it works surprisingly well, at least based on the latest reviews.

Swim Drills Every Triathlete Must Know

So, now you've learned how to swim. The next question you have is, "how can I train for the swim leg of the triathlon?"

Just doing laps at the local pool is okay but it won't dramatically improve your swim performance until you try to do something differently. By differently, we mean trying to address your weak areas. If you did poorly on the water, there must be something wrong in your stroke that can be addressed by more structured training.

Before we get to the actual lap work on the pool, consider the following drills that you need to perform to improve your swim form:

- **Side kicks.** Side kicks are basically drills where you rotate your hips to the side and adapt a side-ward position akin to a coin standing upright on the ground. To make yourself as streamlined as possible, tuck your head into your armpits and extend one arm out in front. Try to kick to move forward and breathe every 5-6 kicks by turning your head towards the ceiling.

    Check out this video to learn more about side kicks.

    https://www.youtube.com/watch?v=0mjZsk8L0M0&feature=youtu.be

- **One-arm stroke.** This is ideal if you want to target a specific element of your swim stroke that's weaker than all the others. It's basically swimming but only pulling on one arm while the other remains straight out in front. Here's another video on YouTube to help you become more familiar with one-arm stroke drills.

https://www.youtube.com/watch?v=hICK_CVeoow&feature=youtu.be

- **Pull buoy drills.** We've already talked about this one. Put a pull buoy in between your legs either at the calf area or at the thigh and do swim laps on the pool like you normally would except for the fact that you now should not move your legs. Don't worry, the pull buoy will help you remain in the right position and allow you to float but with this drill, you'll be mostly working your upper body to improve your pull in the water.

- **Hand paddle drills.** You can do this with or without a pull buoy, depending on your needs and preference. For this drill, just swim as you would but this time wearing hand paddles. You'll feel the additional resistance from the water and that can help build your upper body strength to improve your catch.

Swim-Specific Workouts for a Strong Swim Base

Just as you will find in the next chapter to help improve your cycling endurance, consider using this swim training template to help improve your endurance, speed and form in the water. (See table on page 18.)

	400m	800m	1200m
Endurance	**Warm-up** 4x25 **Main Set** *Drill* 2x25 pull *Ladder* 25, 50, 50, 25 **Cool-down** 2x25	**Warm-up** 1x25, 1x50, 1x75 **Main Set** *Drill* 2x25 pull 2x25 kick *Ladder* 25, 50, 75, 100, 75, 50, 25 **Cool-down** 1x75, 1x50, 1x25	**Warm-up** 2x50, 1x100 **Main Set** *Drill* 2x50 as 25 right arm, 25 left arm 2x50 or 4x25 kick *Ladder* 50, 100, 150, 150, 100, 50 **Cool-down** 1x100, 2x50
Form	**Warm-up** 4x25 **Main Set** *Drill* 2x25 right arm 2x25 pull 2x25 left arm 2x25 kick 2x25 catch up **Cool-down** 2x25	**Warm-up** 1x25, 1x50, 1x75 **Main Set** *Drill* 3x25 right arm 3x25 pull 3x25 left arm 3x25 kick 3x25 catch up *Swim* 3x50 easy (focus on technique) **Cool-down** 2x50, 1x25	**Warm-up** 2x50, 1x100 **Main Set** *Drill* 4x25 right arm 4x25 pull 4x25 left arm 4x25 kick 4x25 catch up *Swim* 3x100 easy (focus on technique) **Cool-down** 1x100, 2x50
Speed	**Warm-up** 4x25 **Main Set** 8x25 (hard with long recovery) **Cool-down** 4x25	**Warm-up** 2x25, 2x50 **Main Set** 12x25 (hard with long recovery) 4x50 (hard with long recovery) **Cool-down** 2x50, 2x25	**Warm-up** 2x50, 1x100 **Main Set** 12x25 (hard with long recovery) 10x50 (hard with long recovery) **Cool-down** 1x100, 2x50

Here are some tips to using the template:

- First, consider your schedule and make sure you spend enough time with swimming workouts. For beginners, it is advisable to do 3 to 4 shorter workouts per week as opposed to 2 long workouts so you can hold the form better with more repetitions. This is also a great way to prevent boredom and keep you excited for the next sessions. With that said, if you know you'll keep to 2 sessions a week whilst 3 or 4 sessions might result in you dropping out, stick to 2 sessions. Ask yourself which option will result in you doing more swimming during your training cycle.

- Second, picture your target workout distance as indicated in the column headings. If you are training for an Olympic distance triathlon, use the 1,200-meter column and so on.

- Third, I would recommend doing two form workouts and one endurance workout per week. For the speed workout, try to do one about every 2 to 3 weeks. If you can do four sessions a week, try adding one more endurance session for the fourth day. Make sure to focus on just one aspect per training day and not mix and match workouts so you can target specific needs and improve your swim faster.

- Here's a quick guide on the terms used for this template:
    - Right arm – means you only use your right arm and a pull buoy to keep you afloat. This is basically a one-arm drill with just your right arm.
    - Left arm – this should be self-explanatory
    - Pull – use a pull buoy and train your arm stroke while your feet remain steady.
    - Kick – use a kickboard and train your kick motion while your arms remain steady.
    - Catch-up – use a pull buoy and try to complete one stroke on one arm before you do the stroke on the other arm.

More Swimming Tips

You can never have too many swimming tips. The swim is easily one of the most technical – and also most chaotic – part of triathlon. It doesn't help that the swim course tends to be the most unpredictable; one minute the water is flat, the next minute you're look at sizable waves.

The "mass start" of most triathlons also complicates things as we'll discuss in a bit.

So yes, you can never have too many swimming tips to help you succeed. Here are some of the key ones. See which ones you can embrace quickly and apply during your next training and/or race.

1. The freestyle is the most important stroke in triathlon swimming. It's the most efficient but this does not mean you should forget all other strokes. The backstroke, for example, can be important if you're trying to recover your breath but you need to keep moving. The breaststroke can also be invaluable if you just need to relax and recover because you've lost confidence in your freestyle and need some time to recover.

   You will ultimately rely on your freestyle to get you to the end of the swim but having other swim strokes in your arsenal can help you become a more confident swimmer, and that means you're better prepared to deal with all the chaos that ensues during the mass start. It also makes training more fun when you vary the strokes.

2. Speaking of mass start, the honest truth is that nothing can prepare you for what happens when the gun goes off. People get kicked and kick back; people punch, people claw their way and encounter all sorts of troubles along the way.

If you're a relatively slow swimmer, try to stay at the back of the pack and take your time starting. If you stay at the front, more people will end up catching you and that's bad news for trying to find a clean path. By staying at the back, you can allow the crowd to thin a little bit and you'll have more room for doing your thing.

Conversely, try to stay at the front if you are a fast swimmer. The reason for that should be pretty obvious from the previous paragraph. If the thought of a mass start is off putting, you can sign up to triathlons with swimming pool 'swim' sections until you feel more confident.

3. Practice sighting. Sighting refers to your ability to direct and re-direct yourself as you swim. It's not easy trying to keep a straight line in the water and your failure to do so can lead to all sorts of tragedy including the eventual outcome where you swim a much longer distance than what the course requires. You don't want to swim more than you have to so try to literally keep an eye on where you're going.

   The best way to do this is to practice looking up but doing so within the limitations of your swim stroke. You wouldn't want to completely stop mid-swim to find where you are and then swim again. That's time-consuming and also tiring. Practice sighting in the pool and then practice again in open water and you'll be able to develop a smoother strategy eventually.

4. That last part is important: don't be contented with swimming in the pool. At some point, you'll have to transition to open water. Most races are in open water and if you haven't tried it before, it can be daunting. Like most challenges, break it down into manageable chunks and

gradually expose yourself to open water until you get used to it.

One of the things that will help your confidence is to practice your treading water technique. Treading is when you stay still in the water and still float at the same time. During the first few instances when you try to swim in open water, the change in environment can be difficult and some swimmers can feel a bit of anxiety. It's good to be confident enough in your swim skills that you know you can just relax and regain your composure before you go again. This is where treading can be an extremely valuable tool for you to keep your nerves in control and just keep going. The more practice you can get of open water swimming, the less daunting it will come race day. Don't ever swim alone in open water. Make sure you practice in a safe environment with qualified coaches. There are open water or triathlon training locations all over the world.

Transition 1 Training Tips

Now we come to the last part of the swim, the transition. If you haven't known it yet, the change from the swim to the bike is known as Transition 1 or T1 while the change from the bike to the run is T2.

The unfortunate truth is that many athletes focus too much on T2 but not do enough training for T1. Getting out of the water will force your body to adjust. You'll feel yourself a bit heavier than usual, even lethargic. You won't immediately have your legs underneath you. You'll probably even be out of breath from the swim and you'll quickly find yourself a bit dazed heading to the transition area.

So let's address this situation by planning and practicing your T1 routine properly.

First, the actual transition.

You'll need to get out of your swim gear and into your bike gear. To do this, follow a protocol – try to go foot to head or head to foot depending on your preference. This progressive sequence allows you to check that you have all that you need and you don't end up missing anything.

Let's simulate a head-to-foot routine to get you into the scheme of things.

- Start out by putting on your bike helmet.

- Put on your sunglasses if you use one during the bike, or check that you have it with you if you don't want to put it on yet.

- Put on your t-shirt/top with race number attached. It's better if you're using a race belt without a t-shirt/top so you can just quickly slip it on. If you're not using a race belt, make sure the number is pinned onto your race top before the race. You don't want to be trying to pin it on your shirt at the transition area.

- Put on socks. You'll probably need a towel to dry off first before you can get your socks on properly. If you're the type to use compression socks during the bike leg, make sure you practice putting it on with your feet a bit wet to simulate the exact race condition. Also, don't use new compression socks that haven't been stretched yet on race day. New socks are tough to put on and that can shave off minutes on your total time.

- Put on your cycling shoes. At this point, we wouldn't recommend that you try the old triathlon trick of leaving the shoes on your bike and putting them on as you ride, unless you practiced this beforehand. It's harder than it looks!

Make sure you do this routine several times in practice so you can have a mental map in your head on how to do it. Doing it the first time on race day can lead to nasty blunders; you wouldn't want that to derail your first triathlon race. Treat T1 like any other part of your training. Practice, time yourself, look for inefficiencies, and repeat.

Now, the next part: swim-bike transitions (BRICK sessions).

Again, many athletes don't do this enough in training. These sessions are essential if you want to get into the thick of things immediately. Once you've practiced your T1 routine, you can start piecing it all together. As a basic workout, we recommend doing two to four laps at the local pool, then jumping into transition 1, and then out to a 5-kilometer short ride. Try to do this a few times in training so you can pick up the feeling better. You don't have to be too systematic about this as you would the bike-run BRICK sessions later on but having some experience in training to use as reference can be valuable for your racing success.

In addition, don't forget to do light swim-run transitions as well. In some races, you might have to run up to half a kilometer to get from the water to T1. Running on weak legs is a pain and you'll need to do some training to make sure you can run after a swim. You don't have to be too fancy about this but, say, two to four laps in the pool plus a half kilometer run afterwards would be a good start.

BRICK sessions are important for all triathlon distances and for many reasons. First of all, they give you first hand experience of what the transitions feel like (how your mind and body adjust). The best training in any sport is race/match specific, you can't get more specific than going through the transitions. In one training session. They also keep your training interesting, challenging and fun. Doing these sessions 2-3 times every other week should set you up for your first triathlon adventure.

Chapter in Summary

The swim portion is often a major cause of worry for many athletes but it does not have to be so. You can train for the swim, and if you are weak in it, then you only need to train more often. Check out the drills and the swim training template we included to help you fix your form, endurance, and speed. These might not seem like much but if you do them regularly, you'll be a capable swimmer in no time!

CHAPTER 3. THE BIKE

The second leg of the triathlon has to do with completing the bike leg.

Again, just like in the swim leg, we're going to assume that you already have basic bike skills. If you don't know how to ride a bike, you're going to have to find someone who can teach you how to do it.

As soon as you're ready, come back and we'll get started with discussing the basics of the cycling leg that will see you through from the mount line off of to the run.

Cycling Gear

Now, on to the exciting part for a lot of people: the cycling gear.

Here's a list of the most important equipment that you will need to complete the bike leg.

The Bike

The bike is your most important equipment during the cycling leg. But what constitutes a good bike and what should you think of having in order to complete the cycling portion without problems?

Here are a few things you should think about.

Firstly, I would recommend that you figure out what type of triathlon race you are doing. While most triathlons are done on paved roads, there are a few like the XTERRA series that are done on trails. The XTERRA series, and other off-road triathlons, require that you use a mountain bike.

On the other hand, the typical triathlon races that you'll find will almost always need a road bike or a triathlon bike. Some of these races still allow the use of mountain bike and if you are only after finishing your first, a mountain bike can be more than sufficient to get you to the run.

But if you are a bit more competitive, you might want to consider getting a road bike or a triathlon bike. To delve deeper into this discussion, let's first look at the different types of bike and their general descriptions so you know how to identify one from the other.

Road Bike. These are the types of bikes you'll see ridden on the Tour de France and other professional cycling races. Below is a picture of a road bike with all the important parts labeled for your reference.

There are many different types of road bikes from different manufacturers and each bike can be made from different materials. The oldest bikes are often made from steel and steel alloys and tend to be generally heavier while the most recent models are either made from aluminum or even full carbon.

There are also other features of the road bike that make it distinct from other bike types. Firstly, you'll notice that the handle bars are sloped downward and in. This design is known as the drop bar and it allows a rider to ride "on the drops" and get into a more aerodynamic position.

Another thing that you can easily notice in road bikes is the narrow profile of the wheels. The wheels are only typically between 23 millimeters to 28 millimeters in width with the 23 mm version being the most common. These wheels are designed in this way because of weight considerations (minimize the weight) as well as reduce the rolling resistance with the road.

Without jumping the gun on the next section about road bike versus triathlon bikes for triathletes, it is important to note that road bikes are generally more versatile and therefore offer more varied riding opportunities than triathlon bikes. Many who are often new to triathlon start out with a road bike and with just a few little tweaks, they can easily convert their bikes to a time trialing setup.

In the next section, we'll dive deeper into the bikes best for triathlon racing and will talk about the ultimate decision on which type of bike to purchase depending on your triathlon goals.

Triathlon Bike. A triathlon bike, or TT bike for short, is a bike specifically designed for "time trialing."

As you can see from the picture, there are obvious differences between a standard road bike and a triathlon bike. The first thing you'll see that's obvious is the handle bar. Gone are the sloped bars and replaced with what is known as a base bar and aero-bar setup.

The second change that is not so obvious to untrained eyes is the angle of the seat tube. Triathlon bikes often come with seat tube angles between 76-78 degrees which is about 4 degrees more than typical road bike seat tube angles.

The combination of the handle bar change with the seat tube angle change leads to a more "aggressive" geometry for triathlon bikes. The concept of the aggressive fit puts the rider on a TT bike into a lower and more aerodynamic position. This allows the rider to ride faster for the same power input because of the lower amount of air resistance that he or she has to overcome while riding.

A more aggressive position, however, comes with its fair share of trade-offs. First, triathlon bikes are mainly designed for straight-line speed so the handling characteristics of a TT bike are not as refined as that of a road bike. Second, comfort might also be an issue for some riders given the aggressive riding position in a triathlon bike; hence, it's not advisable for cyclists who are new to biking to immediately get a TT bike.

All told, serious triathlon enthusiasts and the pros all use triathlon bikes to gain speed. In the next section, we'll dive deeper into whether or not it makes sense for first-time triathletes like you to buy a triathlon bike. This should help you in deciding which type of bike works best for you.

Mountain Bike. Mountain bikes are, as the name implies, bikes built for mountain or trail riding.

There are several features that make mountain bikes easily recognizable from the other types of bikes we've discussed so far. First off, the handle bars tend to be straight to allow for a more upright riding position. This gives the rider better control of the bike which is a requirement when riding trails.

Second, the bike is fitted with "fatter" tires than the ones you'd find on road bikes and triathlon bikes. In mountain bike riding, rolling resistance is not a major concern. Rather, you want the bike to have more traction against the riding surface to improve control and stability.

Third, mountain bikes are often fitted with suspension to facilitate a smoother and more responsive ride even on trails. Mountain bikes can be further classified depending on the type of suspension they have. A bike with both front and back suspension is referred to as a full-suspension or FS bike while a bike which only front suspension is often called a "hard tail."

You will seldom find mountain bikes in road race triathlons but for those races that specially caters to beginners, you will be allowed to race on a mountain bike.

This brings us to an interesting subject that will cross your mind more than a few times as you begin your triathlon journey: which type of bike should you get and use on race day?

Road bike vs TT bike: Which One Should You Get?

Let's start off by saying you need to check with your chosen race if there are limitations in the type of bike you can use on race day. If you have a mountain bike and it is allowed, we highly recommend that you stick with the bike you are already comfortable with. True, you'll lose some time on race day to riders on a road bike or TT bike but if your goal is simply to try out the triathlon scene and see if it's for you, then a mountain bike would suffice. Put simply, we would not recommend going out to purchase a road bike or TT bike if you're only going to use it once or twice and then move on from triathlon racing. That's just not practical.

Now, suppose you are really committed to triathlon and you have money to burn; do you get a road bike or a triathlon bike?

The one thing that mainly sets road bikes apart from TT bikes is their versatility. You won't find too many people going out on a fun and leisure ride with friends using a TT bike. We've also already discussed how comfort and handling can be a bit less refined in a TT bike so if you're friends are inviting you out for a ride on a route that features technical descents, your TT bike might be less capable of taking on that challenge.

On the flip side, there is no denying the aerodynamic advantage of a well-designed triathlon bike. If you like to do solo long rides on relatively quiet roads where you can just bow your head into aero and power through, then there is no mistaking that the TT bike is for you. This is also the chosen option for many professional triathletes who mostly do aero riding in preparation for races. As such, if you are truly serious with triathlon racing, a TT bike might be a good investment but only if you understand exactly what you're getting when you get a TT bike over a standard 'roadie'.

Of course, you always have the option to buy both bike types if you have money to burn but the question then is, where's the fun in that?

The best advice I can give you is to think long and hard about your future riding preferences. If you're a cyclist at heart and you want to have long and fun rides with friends, a TT bike is most likely not for you. If, however, you are serious about focusing on triathlon racing and you feel you have it in you to complete a full distance race in the future, buying a TT bike today can pay big dividends in your racing career. Think long and hard about what you want to do in the future and use this to dictate your bike-buying decisions accordingly.

If you're still unsure, start lower and work your way up. Buy or borrow a 'roadie', use it in training and a triathlon race. How does it feel? Stick with a simle option until you know the sport is for you. You're likely to find bigger gains in speed and efficiency from a Mountain Bike to a Road Bike than you will from a Road Bike to a TT bike. You can always buy a TT Bike 6-12 months after you're into the sport. They aren't going anywhere! You can also turn your 'roadie' into a TT bike.

From Roadie to TT: How to Convert your Road Bike into a Time Trial Bike

Just because you purchased a road bike does not mean you'll have to completely lose out on the benefits of an aggressive riding position to gain aerodynamic advantage. On the contrary, there are some things you can do to make your road bike as close enough to being a TT bike as possible.

But first, an exercise.

Can you recall which features of the TT bike make it significantly different from a standard road bike (excluding the geometry of the frame)?

- Aero and base-bar setup instead of drop bar
- Seat tube angle steeper than in a road bike

These are the most obvious differences between a road bike and a triathlon bike and with just a few tweaks and new parts, it's possible to improve the geometry of a road bike to make it more suited to triathlon racing. Consider buying the following new parts if you wish to easily convert your road bike to a time-trial setup and vice versa.

Clip-on Aerobars. Clip-on aerobars are aerobars that you can quickly install on standard drop bars with just a few twists of the bolts.

Installing clip-on aerobars on your road bike allows you to ride in the familiar aero-position with your elbows rested on the pads and your arms directly aligned with your torso.

There are many different designs for aerobars (L-bends, ski-bends, S-bends, etc.) and there's no general rule that allows you to pick one in favor of the others. In the end, it all boils down to comfort and familiarity. It's best that you try out different designs at your local bike shop to find out which one works best for your riding style.

Fast-Forward Seatpost. Getting clip-on aerobars alone is not enough to convert your road bike into a TT setup. The first picture below shows a bike with clip-on aerobars and a standard road bike seat post design.

The seat post basically changes the seat tube angle of a bike from the conventional 72 –degrees to the triathlon standard of 76-78 degrees. This brings the rider closer to the handle bars making the aero position more comfortable. You will also notice that the position of the rider's hips changes with a fast-forward seatpost; the rider now pedals almost on-top of the chain ring and this engages a different set of muscles in the legs which is said to help conserve your leg muscles for the succeeding run leg.

The best part with both of these upgrades is that they are very easy to install and can be done in just a few minutes. With just a bit of practice, you should be able to quickly switch from a standard road bike setup to a time trialing setup by just making the requisite changes.

Getting a Bike Fit

While we're on the subject of setting up your bike to make it work for you, we might as well talk about getting a bike fit.

A bike fit refers to the systematic way of checking and ensuring that your bike "fits" you. Just like you would check to see if a shirt or pants or shoes matches you, a bike also has to be subjected to the same process.

The end goal of a bike fit is to make you comfortable with your riding position so you can ride for hours without unnecessary pain. Remember: riding for hours will naturally lead to pain in some areas but it should not be because you are straining to match yourself to your bike.

For example, you can have pain in your lower back that might be cause by having a frame that's too big or a fit that forces your torso to extend because you are too far from the handle bars. You can also have pain in your shoulders because you're putting too much force on your hands while riding, or pain in your knees and hips because you are overextending or rocking with each pedal stroke.

A bike fit aims to fix all these and make sure that your bike is dialed to the exact specifications that your body requires.

A bike fit can be done by a professional fitter who is trained to perform the fitting process. There are many schools of thought in bike fitting and there can be some disagreements between fitters as to the right way to fit a bike, but the general concepts largely remain the same and the end goal does not change: comfort over aesthetics. I have an example on the next page of a chart that a fitter uses to compare potential adjustments to remedy a specific problem area. Courtesy of www.bikefit.com.

Because you are employing a professional service, bike fitting comes at a cost. The most sophisticated systems like Retul can actually lead to a significant fee while the most basic fitting systems (or services for a fitter) can range from $100 to $150 depending on the area you are in. However, given the potential benefits of a good fit, you can consider that would be a sound investment for any serious triathlete or cyclist.

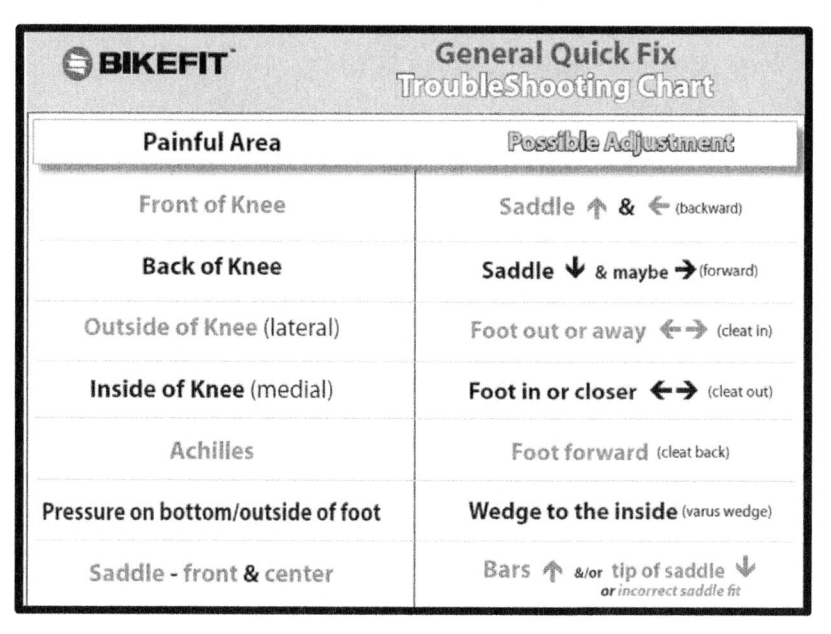

BIKEFIT – General Quick Fix TroubleShooting Chart

Painful Area	Possible Adjustment
Front of Knee	Saddle ↑ & ← (backward)
Back of Knee	Saddle ↓ & maybe → (forward)
Outside of Knee (lateral)	Foot out or away ←→ (cleat in)
Inside of Knee (medial)	Foot in or closer ←→ (cleat out)
Achilles	Foot forward (cleat back)
Pressure on bottom/outside of foot	Wedge to the inside (varus wedge)
Saddle - front & center	Bars ↑ &/or tip of saddle ↓ or incorrect saddle fit

An alternative approach to getting a bike fit is to do it on your own. There are plenty of videos on YouTube that teach DIY bike fitting. There are also plenty of websites that talk about the most important aspects of bike fitting. Many riders who are confident enough in their own skills actually do it this way; besides, bike fitting all boils down to how you feel during a ride. An expert can do all the tweaks but you remain as the best judge of the success of the fit. For this reason, many cyclists try to do the necessary tweaks themselves and test out the results until they get to a fit that they are happy with.

Regardless of your preference, I highly recommend that you spend some time thinking, and doing something, about your bike fit. Racing a triathlon race requires that you spend a lot of time on your bike, and more so if you are going for a longer-distance race. To ensure that you don't experience unnecessary aches and pains that can derail your training routine, a bike fit is a sound investment in both time and money.

Basic Bike Parts and Accessories Every Triathlete Should Know

If you haven't realized it yet, allow me to state the obvious: the bike leg is the most equipment-dependent component of triathlon. You can swim or run or almost close to zero equipment dependency but you cannot do that on the cycling leg. You will only be as successful as your bike – and the corresponding accessories – will take you so it is important to know as much about the essential parts and accessories for your bike as you can.

These are some of the considerations you should spend some time thinking right before you get into the thick of triathlon training.

Clipless Pedals

This is a great topic and I'm sure you'll end up considering this idea more than a few times before you'll eventually come to a decision.

Clipless pedals are pedals specifically designed to interlock with the cleats on your shoe giving you a very solid connection to your bike. Unlike platform pedals where you simply press your shoe on the pedals and push down for each cycle, clipless pedals allow you to derive power during the upward stroke of pedal cycle because now you can "pull up" the pedal. The picture above shows different examples of clipless pedals with the accompanying cleats. The cleat attached to the bottom of your cycling shoes and "clip on" to the pedals to secure the connection. For clarification purposes, a clipless pedal only works if you have the right cycling shoe to pair with it. Remember: the pedals are designed to ensure a solid interlock between your foot and the bike so the shoe is just as important as the pedal. Put simply, the two should be taken as one integral unit for your cycling success. Below is a picture of a cycling shoe with cleats next to clipless pedals for your reference.

While the benefits of going "clipless" in triathlon are obvious – you get to deliver more power per stroke so you can power your bike more efficiently – learning to use clipless pedals can also be a pain. Riders who are used to using platform pedals will immediately have problems with "unclipping" their shoes once they are in motion and need to stop. Many riders have fallen victim to this problem and have crashed as a result. For this reason, it's not advisable to switch to clipless pedals for the first time close to race day as one would need enough practice to get acquainted to the demands of going clipless.

If this is you, then here are some tips that will help prevent you from "tipping over" when using clipless pedals.

Start by practicing the clipping and unclipping motion from a standing position. For this, you need to know what motion is required by your chosen pedal design. Most pedals like the ones from Shimano and Look are unclipped with a twisting motion of the heel and ankles while others like Speedplay unclip if you yank out hard enough. You need to know this first before you even set out to practice because you need to be doing plenty of repetitions before you're ready for a ride.

I recommended clipping in and unclipping out at least 50 times on each foot from a standing position before trying out with the bike in motion.

Once you're ready, you can go ahead and try doing this as you are riding your bike. Make sure to pick an empty street free from vehicles and other potential dangers. Start by clipping one foot in – usually your dominant foot – and pushing down to drive forward. As you are moving, try to see if you can clip in your other foot to completely lock yourself to your bike.

One important reminder: do not try to stop by braking quickly if you are completely locked in on both feet unless you want to try that helpless position of tipping over. You won't like the results.

Now, for the other part of the process: clipping out. Try to unclip from the pedals just as you are lightly applying the brakes to slow down your bike. Often, you will be more comfortable doing this on your non-dominant foot. Time the sequence properly so your foot is out and ready to anchor you just as your bike comes to a stop. Do this a few times before you go out on a ride with clipless pedals.

As a last comment on switching to clipless, make sure that you're alert and aware of what's in-front of you when you're riding. You will need to be quick and coordinated while riding on busy streets clipped on. Try to pre-empt what's going to happen particularly with traffic light situations and vehicles. Again, do not quickly apply the brakes before you've clipped out; manage the brakes and the clipping out process simultaneously to give you enough time to stop properly!

The takeaway: there is no denying the importance of clipless pedals for better efficiency during the cycling leg. Just take time to practice using it. Never try using clipless pedals too close to race day if you want to maximize its benefits and minimize the risk of falling flat on your side.

A great consideration for race day is to clip the shoes onto the pedals prior to the race (without you in them!). Once you've finished the swim leg, you can start riding on top of the shoes and strap your feet into the shoes as you're riding. This takes practice! Please take into account the points above before trying this.

Helmet

Another important accessory to the triathlete's cycling arsenal is a good helmet.

Before we get to the different types of helmets available, it is important to highlight that fit is an overriding consideration for choosing a helmet. Aesthetics mean little if your helmet does not serve its intended purposes, i.e. protect your head from impact forces in the unlikely event of a crash.

Now, let's go to the other considerations for helmet selection.

First up, it is important to highlight that almost all triathlon races require their athletes to wear a helmet. You will never get away with trying to ride your bike without the appropriate protection on your head. If you're one to hate helmets because they are restricting, you have to learn to set this aside and embrace the importance of helmets in cycling and triathlon.

Second, sizing your helmet properly is essential so it can do its intended purpose. A properly-sized helmet will fit snugly on to your head with just a few adjustments. You can play around with the strap and the tightening knob at the back to get the exact fit dialed in. While riding, the helmet should not move about but stay in its place despite taking turns at a high speed.

After taking care of the size, you need to start looking into the material of construction. Most helmets used in competitive cycling and triathlon are made from polystyrene foam because they tend to be lighter without sacrificing function. One thing to remember with helmets is that they are for single-use only as the foam does not recover or bounce back after impact. You should consider immediately replacing your helmet if you had a crash in order to continue ensuring your safety for future rides.

As a last comment on bike helmets, if you're a competitive person who's keen to progress in triathlon, you might want to consider thinking about getting an aero helmet if you want to gain aerodynamic advantage during your ride. Aero helmets tend to be shaped and designed differently than conventional helmets; they feature lesser vent holes and are more streamlined. Studies have shown that they can help shave off a few precious seconds from your overall time, although it has to be said that if you're competing for the first time, the extra investment for an aero helmet is probably overkill. For purposes of completing your first triathlon, a simple and affordable road bike helmet should suffice but if you are serious with competing and want to finish with the best time possible, invest in an aero helmet.

Below are pictures of a standard road bike helmet, an aero-designed roadie helmet, and a full-aero helmet in all its pointy glory.

There is no doubt that the aero helmet looks cooler – and faster – but it all boils down to practicality. It certainly doesn't help if you're on a road bike converted to a tri-setup and you only have an aero helmet to go around.

Why? Because you'd stop looking cool the moment you switch back to a road bike setup for fun rides and all you have is an aero helmet to go with it.

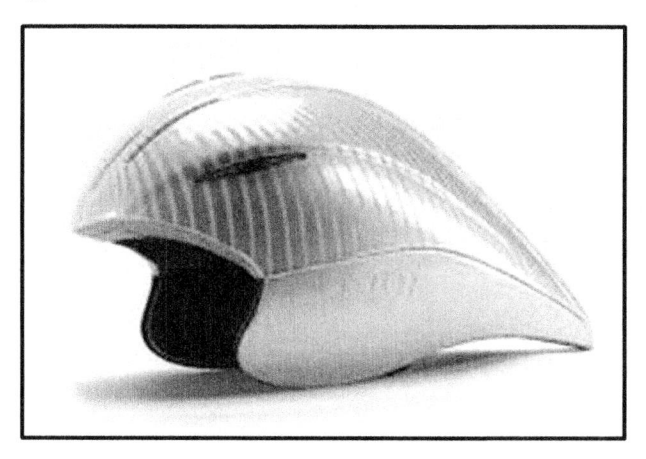

Cycling Tips for Beginners

Before going into the important training details for cycling training, there are a few things you need to take note as a beginner cyclist. Even if you say you've been biking before, cycling in a competitive setting can be nerve-racking and if you're not prepared for it, you might end up having problems on race day.

To avoid this, you need to prepare for a few basic things to help you get through race day.

- Get acquainted with your bike's gears and gearing mechanism. Nowadays, the industry-standard when it comes to gear shifting in road bikes is the STI or Shimano Total Integration which is a fancy way of saying that your brakes and gear shift mechanisms are integrated into one lever. Most lever designs nowadays look the same but there are subtle differences to the way each gear brand handles shifting.

    You need to get acquainted with this as soon as possible. Even if you're just doing a sprint triathlon, try to spend some time on your bike so you can quickly adapt to the demands of your new bike. It will take a couple of weeks of riding before you start to become comfortable so you have to plan for more rides at the onset to get you familiar with the competitive cycling scene.

- If you're riding in a draft-legal race – that means that you're allowed to slip behind other riders to take advantage of their slipstream – you will quickly find yourself riding in a peloton situation. Peloton is the official term used to refer to a bunch or group of cyclists riding together.

Being in a peloton can be nerve-racking if you're not used to doing it. Riding in a group demands that you ride in a predictable manner, that you are responsive to the overall behavior of the group (like a school of fish in the sea, for example), and that you have at least average bike-handling skills so you don't cause anyone to topple over during the ride.

Riding in a peloton requires practice; there's just no two ways about it. You will only get comfortable in a bunch group if you've done it several times. To prepare for this, get some friends to help you be more comfortable in a bunch so you can practice peloton riding to help you conserve more energy during the cycling leg.

- If you are in a none-drafting race, i.e. you are not allowed to stay behind other riders, you will quickly find yourself in a long solo riding situation. This too has its fair share of demands, mostly mental as opposed to physical.

First, you need to learn how to judge your distance from the rider in front of you so you don't get penalized for drafting. The usual rule is to stay about 7 meters behind the rider in front of you and about 2 meters on each side. You are only allowed to ride up on a rider if you have the intention of passing him or her, and even then you'd have to do that quickly so you get out of their slipstream quicker.

Second, you need to get acquainted with solo riding. Biking is fun if you have a group to ride with; it can be mentally taxing if you're doing it alone – and that's the likely scenario that you'll face when it's time to race. Get familiar with this situation by doing some solo rides at distances longer than the cycling leg so you won't get a rude awakening on race day.

- Learn some basic bike fixing skills.

    Perhaps the most important cycling tip you'll ever receive as a beginner is to learn how to do some basic bike fixes without the aid of qualified mechanic. We've seen it quite often; riders new to biking get a bike and completely depend on their mechanic for everything about their bike. On race day, they encounter a situation which requires some basic bike skills and they end up on the side of the road helpless and unable to finish.

    Start out by learning how to change a flat and inflating your tire. This is the most basic problem on race day and one that even the pros are not immune against. A flat tire will catch you at the most inopportune time and you should be quick enough to change and re-inflate within just a few minutes so it does not sabotage your race.

    Other bike repair skills you should learn include re-installing the chain if in case it comes off and adjusting and aligning your brakes. These are very basic skills that do not take a lot of time to learn.

    We recommend you check on GCN or Global Cycling Network on YouTube. They have a lot of great bike repair videos and other tips that can help you become a much better cyclist with just a few minutes of practice. Take the time to practice all of the above before going into a race.

Bike Workouts to Improve your Performance

Now that we've been through the beginner tips, you'll need to do some cycling specific training to help boost your performance. Here are some bike workouts that you need to start doing if you plan to compete in your first triathlon and finish in a respectable time.

First off, try to assess if you'll need a bike trainer. A bike trainer allows you to train indoors so even if you don't have time to go out for a ride, you can still get on your bike even for short interval workouts. Trainers are particularly useful if your work schedule forces you to ride at the worst times, i.e. you come home late at night or you work during the night and you're forced to ride in the middle of the day. Trainers are also great for inclement weather so if you live in an area with nasty winters or frequent rain, trainers will quickly become your bestfriend.

Now, with or without trainers, you'll need to try doing more of these cycling workouts to get you into the right shape for racing your first triathlon.

- **Easy spins.** These are self-explanatory. An easy spin refers to an easy ride, although it probably isn't as easy or as leisurely as you think. Easy spins require you to keep the cadence – the number of revolutions on your pedals – to about 85-92 rpm.

    Important note: At this point, you should consider getting a cyclo-computer with a cadence sensor, although to be honest it's not recommended and many triathletes train without it without a loss in performance.

    The purpose of easy spins is to just get you used to riding your bike. Cyclists will call it saddle time and to be honest, this is essential if you're new to cycling and just trying to get acclimated to being on a road bike or triathlon bike.

- **Intervals.** Intervals are designed to build your speed and you'll need about 2-3 interval sessions per week to build your fitness quickly. A typical interval consists of a short-fast period at 100-105 rpms and a rest period of a couple of minutes to get your heart-rate down before you do it again.

Here's an example of a simple interval workout; 15 x 30-secs at 100 rpms with 1-minute recovery between sets. That means you need to do ride at 100 rpms for 30 seconds, easy spin for 1-minute, and repeat 15 times for a complete workout.

Add a 10-minute warm-up and 5-minute cooldown period and you already have a simple interval workout designed to help you become a better cyclist.

- **Hill climbs.** Hills are the bane of any undertrained cyclist. Nothing can prepare you for hills. You can do a ton of training on the flats at high speeds but because hills require a different set of skills, muscles, and mentality, you can still find yourself crawling on a hill begging for it to end.

For this reason, you cannot discount hill climbs. Find a respectable hill in your area – preferably one that's about 100-200 meters long with a decent gradient of 3-5% and do hill repeats. This means climbing the hill at a steady pace, then coming back down and repeating that again for 8-12 times depending on your fitness level and objective.

Hill climbs are hell for beginner cyclists but if you train for them, you'll undoubtedly do better on race day.

- **One-leg workouts.** This one requires a trainer; you can't do this on the road and expect to get away with it.

For one leg workouts, the objective is to pedal on just one leg at a time to eliminate imbalances between your left and right leg. We all have a dominant leg and in cycling, that can cause problems. To remedy the imbalance, alternate 30-60 seconds with just one leg and aim to do 8-10 minutes per leg in total. You can also alternate between each leg to allow it to rest.

- **Aerobic training.** These are the long ride days when you can just enjoy the scenery and have a blast with friends. Try to do at least 1 hour of long ride every weekend but if you can do more, then all the better.

One Month Cycling Fitness Program

Here's a program I got from www.beginertriathlete.com for cycling training for beginners. Take note that you should try to do this first before you do your triathlon-specific training. In short, consider this a base program that will prepare you for finishing your first or succeeding races.

If you are pressed for time and can't do this in the weeks leading up to your triathlon program, prioritize the comprehensive triathlon training and aim to do this before you race your next triathlon. Remember, a solid foundation can help you finish faster and with lesser pain so if you are serious with racing, you'll find time to build your base before you decide to race again.

Week 1

Day	Duration	Workout
Monday	30'	10' warm up and then 10x30" at 100 rpms with 1' recovery between sets. Cool down for 5' after the last rep.
Tuesday	30'	30' easy spin, keep the effort conversational and the cadence between 85-92 RPMS.
Wednesday	48'	15' warm up. Then 4x4' at 55-65 RPMS. Recovery is 3' easy spinning between sets. Easy 5' cool down.
Thursday	30'	30' easy spin, keep the effort conversational and the cadence between 85-92 RPMS.
Friday	0	Off day – cross train – walk, hike, swim. Nothing strenuous.
Saturday	30"	TRAINER: Warm up 10'. After warm up, alternate 20-60" with 1 leg off the pedals and up on a chair. Get a total of 5' on each leg in workout. Alternate legs as you feel like it. Focus on eliminating dead spot at top of stroke by pushing toes forward in shoes at top. Cool down for 10'.
Sunday	45'	Long aerobic day – ride from 45-75', as you feel.

' refers to the number of minutes
" refers to the number of seconds

Week 2

Monday	38'	10' warm up and then 15x30" at 100 rpms with 1' recovery between sets. Cool down 5' after the last rep.
Tuesday	40'	40' easy spin, keep the effort conversational and the cadence between 85-92 RPMS.
Wednesday	52'	15' warm up. Then 4x5' at 55-65 RPMS. Recovery is 3' easy spinning between sets. Easy cool down for 5'.
Thursday	30'	30' easy spin, keep the effort conversational and the cadence between 85-92 RPMS.
Friday	0	Off day – cross train – walk, hike, swim. Nothing strenuous.
Saturday	35"	TRAINER: 10' warm up. After WU, alternate 30-60" with 1 leg off the pedals, and up on a chair. Get a total of 7' on each leg in workout. Alternate legs as you feel like it. Focus on eliminating dead spot at top of stroke by pushing toes forward in shoes at top. Cool down for 10'.
Sunday	55'	Long aerobic day – ride from 55-75', as you feel.

' refers to the number of minutes
" refers to the number of seconds

Week 3

Day	Duration	Workout
Monday	33'	10' warm up and then 10x45" at 105 rpms with 1' recovery between sets. Cool down for 5' after the last rep.
Tuesday	40'	40' easy spin, keep the effort conversational and the cadence between 85-92 RPMS.
Wednesday	56'	15' warm up. Then 4x6' at 55-65 RPMS. Recovery is 3' easy spinning between sets. Easy cool down for 5'.
Thursday	40'	40' easy spin, keep the effort conversational and the cadence between 85-92 RPMS.
Friday	0	Off day – cross train – walk, hike, swim. Nothing strenuous.
Saturday	35"	TRAINER: Warm up 10'. After WU, alternate 45-60" with 1 leg off the pedals, and up on a chair. Get a total of 7' on each leg in workout. Alternate legs as you feel like it. Focus on eliminating dead spot at top of stroke by pushing toes forward in shoes at top. Cool down for 10'.
Sunday	60'	Long aerobic day – ride from 60-80', as you feel.

' refers to the number of minutes
" refers to the number of seconds

Week 4

Monday	36'	10' warm up and then 12x45" at 105 rpms with 1' recovery between sets. Cool down for 5' after the last rep.
Tuesday	45'	45' easy spin, keep the effort conversational and the cadence between 85-92 RPMS.
Wednesday	60'	15' warm up. Then 4x6' at 55-65 RPMS. Recovery is 3' easy spinning between sets. Easy cool down for 5'.
Thursday	40'	40' easy spin, keep the effort conversational and the cadence between 85-92 RPMS.
Friday	0	Off day – cross train – walk, hike, swim. Nothing strenuous.
Saturday	35"	TRAINER: Warm up 10'. After WU, alternate 50-75" with 1 leg off the pedals, and up on a chair. Get a total of 7' on each leg in workout. Alternate legs as you feel like it. Focus on eliminating dead spot at top of stroke by pushing toes forward in shoes at top. Cool down 10'.
Sunday	70'	Long aerobic day – ride from 70-85', as you feel.

' refers to the number of minutes
" refers to the number of seconds

Transition 2 Training Tips

We've come to the last part of the cycling and biking section but it's perhaps the most important, and that's not an exaggeration.

Okay, let's take care of the easy part first.

The easy part is to plan your transition from bike to run properly. This requires establishing a routine that you can practice multiple times before the race. Take note of the following important considerations at T2:

- Most races require that you rack your bike properly. Failure to do this will result in a penalty. Practice racking up your bike on the type of rack that will be used on race day so you don't spend an inordinate amount of time fidgeting with your bike – and scratching it in the process – before you finally succeed in racking it.

- Some races require that you complete racking your bike before you can take off your helmet. Check if your next race has this as a rule and establish your routine accordingly.

- Figure out if you want a head-to-foot approach or the reverse. Having a direction for fixing your transition helps you eliminate potential mistakes. If you're going to foot-to-head as is common in many triathletes, it means you need to do the following:

- Figure out if you're using compression socks or calf compression and if you want to put them on after the swim or after the bike. Obviously, if you plan to use compression socks after the bike, they'll be your first order of business right after you rack your bike and take off your helmet.

- Change from your cycling shoes to your running shoes.

- Get your race bib number on. If you're using a race belt, you can just turn around your race bib to the front.

- If you run with sunglasses and a cap or visor on, you can just slip on to them while you're running out of the transition area.

- I can't emphasize this enough but you have to practice your transition properly. Many first time triathletes forget about the transition and end up getting confused on race day. Don't allow yourself to fall into this trap. Practice and get your T2 routine in order so you'll be confident and structured on race day.

With the easy part out of the way, it's time to talk about the more important component of Transition 2: BRICK! BRICK is basically the term used by triathletes to describe the transition from one sport into another. For example, the bike into the run or as explained earlier, the swim into a bike ride.to run.

The whole concept of BRICK workouts is all about preparing your body for the change in sport. In T2, it's about preparing your legs to run after you've done the bike. Trust me when I say this part isn't easy for beginners. Just as you tend to struggle transitioning from the swim to the bike leg (because your body tends to feel heavier coming out of the water), your legs will also tend to feel heavy after the bike.

This is where BRICK workouts come in handy.

In its simplest form, BRICK workouts are basically workouts where you string biking and running one after the other. The purpose is to build muscle memory and neural pathways that will allow your body to treat this transition as second nature. Without practicing this routine, you'll end up struggling through a majority of the run leg before your body starts to recover enough for you to run at your preferred pace.

As a point of emphasis, remember this: no matter how hard you train on the run, if you don't train for the transition, you'll end up with dead legs for the first few kilometers. A bike/run BRICK session is designed to condition your legs to recover faster from the bike and on to the run.

So, how can you do your brick workouts?

There are many ways to do this but here's one that you can easily do:

If you have a trainer, setup your bike and trainer beside the track. This will allow you to quickly transition from bike to run and vice versa with minimal fanfare.

Start out on the bike and do a 20-30 minute trackside warm-up. Do this at a decent pace, preferably in the 95-100 rpm range. Once you're warmed up, hop off the bike and change into your running shoes for the track workout. Try to settle into your race pace as quickly as you can and then hold this pace for 3-laps good for 1.2 kilometers.

Repeat this cycle 4 more times for 5 reps in total good for 6 kilometers of running. Finish by cooling down on the bike for 10-15 minutes at an easy spin to allow your legs to recover.

If you don't own a trainer and you're not near an oval track, you can still do this workout if you can pick a convenient setting. You can setup your transition area in your garage or at an empty parking lot and simulate the bike and run reps to get your legs accustomed to the effort.

You can read more about BRICK workouts online and get more ideas about how to perform BRICK sessions. Ideally, you should have a couple of BRICK workouts per week so you can quickly get acclimated to T2 as soon as possible.

Chapter in Summary

The bike leg in a triathlon needs its fair share of training and a whole bunch of equipment to consider. However, it can also be the most fun leg especially if you love being on your bike and going fast.

We recommend spending some time trying to pick up the nuances of triathlon cycling by reviewing this chapter, and then building your cycling fitness with the 1-month plan attached to get you up to speed with the demands of riding your bike and getting ready for a triathlon. After that, you can then transition into your normal triathlon program with a solid cycling base in place.

We also recommend that you seriously think about BRICK workouts from the bike to the run, and to practice your transitions so you don't get caught unaware on race day.

CHAPTER 4. THE RUN

Many consider the run in triathlon as perhaps the easiest discipline but this can be misleading and is often a wrong assumption.

Consider: you've already done the swim and just finished the bike leg; now, you have to run. For many, running is easy but the equation changes when you need to start running after you've done a few other sporting disciplines. For others, running is hard enough as it is and then you now have to do it post-swim and bike.

Regardless of your previous running background, running is undoubtedly the most demanding leg in triathlon. Many races are won or lost on the run. During the 2014 Ironman World Championships in Kona, Hawaii, women's champion Mirinda Carfrae came back from a 14.5-minute deficit off of the bike to run a 2:50:26 marathon and win by more than 2 minutes over the next competitor.

And even if you don't plan on winning your next triathlon race, that still doesn't mean you should take the run lightly. Because it is the last discipline that you need to finish, you are most likely spent when the run leg rolls around. Many who take the run for granted end up walking a majority of the run course and that's no fun way to finish a triathlon, much less your first. You need to prepare the most for it because you'd be tired at this point during the race and that's where sound training can help you power through.

I wrote a book on running your first marathon and many of the tips there apply here. I recommend you get that as well and challenge yourself to completing your first marathon some day.

In parallel, let's look at the things you'd need to know to ace the run leg during your first triathlon race.

Running Gear

Let's start by talking about essential running gear.

Running Shoes

Running shoes are a runner's best friend. Your feet get a lot of pounding during running and the least you can do is offer it some protection by buying the proper running shoes.

But what constitutes "proper" when it comes to running shoes?

Here are a few considerations.

1. Foot Type and Gait Analysis.

   Always start with the proper foot and gait analysis. A shoe may feel good when you walk around the shoe store, it may be pretty with all the great colors, and it may be the cheapest so you immediately buy it without second thoughts, but those things mean nothing if you can't run 2 kilometers into the run leg.

   Your foot type and subsequent gait analysis is the best way to ensure that you're getting the right shoe for your specific needs. For example, if you are flat-footed, then you definitely require a different type of running shoe to runners with a higher arch in their feet. That's because your arch profile dictates how your foot accommodates the impact forces during the run, so the corresponding cushioning will be required to deal with this.

In addition, runners who pronate or supinate – the terms used to describe the way the ankles roll upon impact – also require a different type of shoe according to the locations where the support and cushion are placed. If you pick the wrong shoe, there's a good chance you end up with an injury because your feet are not protected in the right way.

Bottom line, it's prudent to head to the nearest running store in your area and have your gait and foot type analyzed. Many running stores actually offer this service for free, plus they also allow you to run with certain shoes in their line so you can actually test out the shoe in a dynamic setting. I recommend doing this early on so you don't subject yourself to higher injury risks as you train. Getting the shoe right will give you more time to train with the right shoes and that will give you the best chance of injury-free triathlon success.

2. Comfort

   Comfort can mean different things to different people. But there are a few things that should help you select the most comfortable shoe for your needs.

   The first thing you have to consider is shoe design. Some shoes have narrower profiles which can lead to a constricting feeling at the toes or at the arch. Others have wider profiles which can also be uncomfortable during running.

   The material of construction also matters a lot when it comes to comfort. Harder materials with reduced ventilation are especially difficult to use because they can be stiff and rigid. On the flipside, soft materials can also feel wobbly as you run because they tend to offer less support particularly when you run at higher speeds.

And then there is the issue of color which might not seem like much but when it comes to comfort, it can also be a factor; after all, who likes to run in shoes that they don't like visually?

These are just some of the things that you need to consider when picking the right shoe for your triathlon training and racing needs.

3. Test your shoe in race conditions

    One last consideration for selecting the right shoe is to be able to test it before you finalize the purchase. We've already mentioned how some local running shops have a treadmill that can allow you to test the shoe under dynamic conditions; if you have that in your area, try to take advantage of that.

    If you order online, you should look for retailers that allow you to return the product or exchange it for another so you'll be able to test it out for a few days once the product arrives.

    In addition to these considerations, also think about the following to make sure you put your shoe in the best use possible.

    First, think about having more than just one pair of shoes for your training. While it is not prudent to use a new pair first time during the race, it is beneficial to have two to three pairs that you can interchange while training. Different pairs of shoe – provided they are of the correct fit – can help strengthen your feet and make you a better runner overall.

    You should also pay attention to your shoe mileage and have a conscious decision to replace your running kicks every 300 to 400 miles. Impact forces and repetitive use degrades your shoe and over time, it loses its ability to protect your feet properly. Track your shoe mileage and buy a new pair ahead of time so you don't unnecessarily subject your feet to impact forces that can lead to serious running injuries.

Running apparel

Next to the color, which is undoubtedly the most important consideration for picking the right running apparel….

Just kidding!

The thing with picking the right running apparel for triathlon racing is that the demands have changed a little bit and you now need to be mindful of planning for and accommodating all three sports in one go. So let's look at the demands of each sport and see what you can do about it.

- **Swim.** Even if you end up using a wetsuit, there's a very good chance you'll end up wet, so that means finding a material that dries up quickly once you get out of the water. The last thing you need is to be wet the whole way while on the bike, cruising along at 35 km/h and encountering some nasty winds along the way. Chill; that's not cool!

- **Bike.** On the bike, you will need shorts with some level of padding to keep you comfortable. Even if you say you're only going for a 20-km bike ride, which is the standard distance in a sprint triathlon, that will still put you on the road for about 45 minutes or thereabouts. In addition, you also need to wear something that's tight and doesn't flap in the wind. You wouldn't want to work too hard pedalling and lose all that power to wind resistance.

- **Run.** What makes you comfortable on the bike can be a problem area in the run. Try running in full cycling shorts and you'll quickly know what I mean. Extra padding on your shorts can feel like you're running on diapers and nobody wants that. In addition, you can't have too much padding because that will just soak up moisture in the swim and that's not cool either. In short, you need the right amount of padding to remain comfortable but made from a material that doesn't soak up moisture and is not too thick that you'd feel like you're running with diapers.

Enter the tri suit.

Some people have a problem with wearing stretchable materials but you will quickly see that this is the most efficient apparel you can pick for triathlon racing. Tri suits are specifically designed to be streamlined so you cut through the water and the air during the swim and bike legs, dries quickly so it doesn't get heavy after the swim and also when you sweat during the bike and run, and is padded just enough to make you comfortable on the saddle for long bike rides.

I've provided some examples of single-piece triathlon suits from famous sporting apparel maker 2XU. There are also many other manufacturers that supply triathlon suits of all shapes and sizes, plus you will also find two-piece triathlon suits with the top and shorts separate.

A popular option nowadays is to find a local triathlon team willing to take on new members. Local triathlon teams design their own tri suits and that makes it more stylish and colorful than standard offerings by apparel manufacturers. If you can find a local club that will take you in, they can show you the basics of triathlon apparel – as well as coach you about triathlon training and racing – and that can go a long way into boosting your confidence and improving your racing day finishing times.

As a last comment on running apparel or triathlon apparel, you might want to consider the requisite accessory to help you race better. This is where the discussion of compression socks or calf compression comes into play. There is some debate as to the effectiveness of compression apparel for enhancing performance. Some athletes swear by compression apparel and studies have shown that the right compression gear can help delay the onset of cramps and keep your muscles engaged for longer. It's a personal choice both from a performance and style standpoint, but you should think about it more especially if you plan to race at longer distances where cramps and other problems can start to become more of a concern. After all, any advantage that you can get out of something you can wear will go a long way into helping you finish strong.

As a last note, consider using a running cap or visor depending on the weather. Visors can help shade you from the sun while venting your head to keep you cool. For colder weather racing, a running cap might be a suitable option depending on your preferences. Once again, try running in a cap or visor in training prior to the race itself to make sure you're comfortable with it.

Gadgets

Given the multi-sport nature of triathlon racing, we recommend looking into getting a gadget that can help you train effectively in all three disciplines. Your first option would be triathlon specific watches such as the ones designed by Timex, Garmin, Polar, and Suunto among others.

So, how can these gadgets help you train and race better?

The important idea to consider here is learning how to pace yourself properly. There's an adage in business that says "you cannot improve that which you cannot measure." In athletic performance, that adage also holds significance.

How can you expect to run, bike, or swim faster if you don't know how fast you are going in the first place?

A dependable gadget will allow you to monitor your pace and more as you train and race. Gadgets nowadays are equipped with GPS watches making them highly accurate in tracking distance, pace, and even elevation changes. This allows you to track how far you've swam, biked, or ran. It also gives more real-time feedback on how you're doing in terms of instantaneous speed or even heart rate and intensity. Because you can track your training performance, you can train more efficiently and that's the key to improving your fitness.

If you choose not to invest on gadgets that's not a problem (they're really not that cheap), you also have the option to use your smartphone through apps like Nike+, Endomondo, Strava, Runtastic and many others. There are also triathlon-specific apps like Training Peaks that can help you track your training better. Many of these apps come at a cost but if you are serious with your triathlon career, an investment in this area will generally help you be more conscious and measured in your training.

Buying gadgets is not a requisite for triathlon success but it has its fair share of benefits. In the end, you need to find the right balance between spending and still being effective at a reasonable cost and that's something that only you can decide as a newbie triathlete.

Triathlete Running Workouts

With the essential things like apparel and gadgets out of the way, let's now talk about run-specific training.

These are the types of running you should plan on doing to help you improve your run times. You should plan to incorporate these workouts in your regular training schedule so you can take advantage of the benefits of each training type.

- **Speedwork.** If you are aiming to finish your first triathlon in a fast time, you need to add more speedwork to your training. Speed workouts aim to improve your overall pace by forcing your body to get used to running at a higher pace than you are normally used to doing.

One classic example of a speed workout that you can do at the local track involves running 8 repetitions of 400-meters with 2-minute rest intervals afterwards. Try to run the 400-meter lap at the fastest pace you can sustain for the whole distance without having to slow down towards the end. This isn't the same as running as fast as you can. Do this once a week and try to gradually increase the pace while decreasing the rest period durations as you see an increase in your fitness level. You can also plan to increase the total target reps from 8 to 10 to 12 as you start seeing results.

The whole concept behind speed workouts lies behind the body's amazing ability to adapt and adjust depending on the load. Speed workouts are designed to be at the threshold of what you consider as aerobic training and the rest periods are incorporated so you don't tip over into the anaerobic phase and burn out.

If you are planning to do a sprint distance or Olympic distance race as your first, try to do this speed workout at least once a week and track your body's response to the stimulus.

- **Tempo workouts.** Tempo runs are designed to do two things.

First, you want to do tempo runs to push your body to run for extended periods at a target pace. This teaches mental control and discipline so you eventually learn to pace yourself properly. Second, tempo runs are designed to be test runs, i.e. it can be used to gauge your fitness level and see how far you are from goal.

So, how can you do a tempo run?

Basically, target a distance that is close to the final race distance and see if you can run the whole way (without walking) at slightly slower than your target pace. This is the tricky part; say you want to run at race pace of 6:00 minutes per kilometer. Start with tempo runs at roughly 1 minute slower than your target pace some weeks before race day. As you start seeing results from your speed work, you can gradually increase the pace of your tempo runs closer to race pace. In training, you don't necessarily need to match race pace but if you can come close, say 10-15 seconds per kilometer slower, then you're most likely capable of running at your target pace provided you're not in pain from the previous swim and bike leg.

Again, remember that tempo runs are all about control and consistency. The goal is to discipline yourself to run at a hard but sustainable pace. You'll need this kind of discipline when you're out on race day.

- **Hill repeats.** Remember the "hill scenario" we talked about in the bike leg?

The honest truth is that hills, wherever they may be in a route, can be a killer. They can derail you on the bike and on the run. If you don't prepare for them adequately, you'll find yourself in big trouble on race day.

The best advice you can receive when it comes to dealing with hills is to prepare for them by doing a couple of hill repeats before the race. Find a sizable hill in your training area, preferably one that's about 3-5% in gradient and about

100 to 200 meters long. Run up the hill at your target race pace and jog back down to recover. Do this 8 to 10 times per session and every other week to prepare your legs for the dreaded hills on race day.

- **Long Runs.** For sprint distance triathlons, the long run might not be as important especially if you've ran the run leg target distance in training before.

For longer distance races, you'll need to pepper your weekends with long runs, with the distance progressing on a weekly basis by 10-15% up until you get to around 90% of the target. These should be done at a comfortable and easy pace and should just be about spending time on the road running and getting your legs into the natural motion of running for an extended period.

Chapter in Summary

Now, we've covered all three disciplines in more detail. It's time for you to embrace triathlon training by planning multi-sport workouts together. This will be the topic covered in the succeeding chapter.

For now, remember that running might look like it's the easiest discipline but it really isn't. There are plenty of pitfalls in thinking that running is easy, especially since it's at this point in the race when you're most likely to feel spent and tired.

Think about the basics we've discussed here and make sure you do these recommendations rigorously in training. The BRICK sessions covered in the previous chapter is a particularly good workout to remember to allow you to quickly sink your teeth into the run immediately after T2.

You should also focus your attention on speedwork, tempo and hill repeats if you are planning for a shorter race. It's possible to finish fast in a triathlon especially if you're willing to put in the time in training. Remember this and you're more likely to put yourself in a position to succeed than if you were to completely brush the run aside.

CHAPTER 5. YOUR VERY OWN TRIATHLON TRAINING PLANS

Below are two training plans, one designed to get you ready for a Sprint Distance race in four weeks and another to get you ready for the Olympic Distance in six weeks. Take note that while the swim and cycling-specific training we mentioned are not prerequisites for these, you can get into the training quicker and complete the recommended workouts if you've already ironed out your swim and bike-specific plans.

Four-Week Sprint Distance Training Plan

Use this plan to race a sprint distance triathlon in four weeks. The plan already incorporates essential BRICK sessions so pay attention to the specific segments and try to follow the recommended workouts so you can check all the important components of a holistic training plan.

WEEK 1	SWIM	BIKE	RUN
MON	**SWIM 600M** • Warm Up with 200m free form • 1 x 200m free tempo (45 sec rest) • 1 x 100m free tempo (30 sec rest) • Warm Down with 100m breaststroke and backstroke easy	OFF	OFF
TUES	DAY OFF		
WED	OFF	**RIDE 30 MINUTES** • 30 min easy ride • **Run off bike:** 5 min easy run	OFF
THURS	OFF		**RUN 20 MINUTES** • 6 min run/walk easy • 8 min tempo run • 6 min run/walk easy
FRI	DAY OFF		
SAT	**SWIM 600M** • Warm Up with 200m free form • 2 x 50m hard (20 sec rest) • 2 x 100m free tempo (30 sec rest) • Warm Down with 100m breaststroke and backstroke easy	**RIDE 30 MINUTES** • 10 min easy ride • 8 min temp ride • 2 min easy ride • 5 min hard ride • 5 min easy ride • **Run off bike:** 8 min easy run	OFF
SUN	OFF		**RUN 20 MINUTES** • 2 min walk • 16 min easy run • 2 min walk

WEEK 2	SWIM	BIKE	RUN
MON	**SWIM 600M** • Warm Up with 200m free form • 1 x 200m free tempo (45 sec rest) • 1 x 100m free tempo (30 sec rest) • Warm Down with 100m breaststroke and backstroke easy	OFF	OFF
TUES	DAY OFF		
WED	OFF	**RIDE 40 MINUTES** • 10 min easy ride • 10 min tempo ride • 2 min easy ride • 8 min hard ride • 4 min easy ride • **Run off bike:** 10 min easy run	OFF
THURS	OFF		**RUN 25 MINUTES** • 8 min run/walk easy • 9 min tempo run • 8 min run/walk easy
FRI	DAY OFF		
SAT	**SWIM 700M** • Warm Up with 200m free form • 2 x 50m hard (20 sec rest) • 3 x 100m free tempo (30 sec rest) • Warm Down with 100m breaststroke and backstroke easy	**RIDE 40 MINUTES** • 40 min easy ride • **Run off bike:** 5 min easy run	OFF
SUN	OFF		**RUN 25 MINUTES** • 2 min walk • 21 min easy run • 2 min walk

WEEK 3	SWIM	BIKE	RUN
MON	**SWIM 1000M** • Warm Up with 200m free form • 2 x 50m free hard (20 sec rest) • 400m free tempo (60 sec rest) • 2 x 100m free temp (30 sec rest) • Warm Down with 100m breaststroke and backstroke easy	OFF	OFF
TUES	DAY OFF		
WED	OFF	**RIDE 50 MINUTES** • 10 min easy ride • 16 min tempo ride • 4 min easy ride • 10 min hard ride • 10 min easy ride • **Run off bike:** 10 min easy run	OFF
THURS	OFF		**RUN 30 MINUTES** • 6 min run/walk easy • 5 min tempo run • 2 min run/walk easy • 4 min hard run • 2 min run/walk easy • 5 min tempo run • 6 min run/walk easy
FRI	DAY OFF		
SAT	**SWIM 700M** • Warm Up with 200m free form • 2 x 50m hard (20 sec rest) • 3 x 100m free tempo (30m sec rest) • Warm Down with 100m breaststroke and backstroke easy	**45 MINUTE TRANSITION** • 10 min easy ride **Transition Set:** • 8 min hard ride followed by 6 min hard run off the bike. Repeat x 2. • 5 min easy ride	OFF

SUN	OFF	**RUN 30 MINUTES** • 2 min walk • 26 min easy run • 2 min walk

WEEK 4	SWIM	BIKE	RUN
MON	**SWIM 600M** • Warm Up with 200m free form • 2 x 50m free hard (20 sec rest) • 2 x 100m free tempo (30 sec rest) • Warm Down with 100m breaststroke and backstroke easy	OFF	OFF
TUES	DAY OFF		
WED	OFF	**RIDE 30 MINUTES** • 10 min easy ride • 8 min tempo ride • 2 min easy ride • 5 min hard ride • 5 min easy ride **Run off bike:** 8 min easy run	OFF
THURS	OFF		**RUN 20 MINUTES** • 3 min run/walk easy • 4 min tempo run • 2 min run/walk easy • 2 min hard run • 2 min run/walk easy • 4 min tempo run • 3 min run/walk easy
FRI	DAY OFF		
SAT	**SWIM 200M** • Warm Up with 200m free form • 1 x 100m as 25 hard, 25 easy, etc. • Warm Down with 100m breaststroke and backstroke easy	**EASY RIDE 20 MINUTES** • 2 X 1 min Tempo with full recovery	**RUN 3 MINUTES OFF BIKE** • 1 X 30 sec tempo run

SUNDAY – Race Day!

Six-Week Olympic Distance Training Plan

Here's the recommended plan for racing an Olympic distance triathlon in the next six weeks. Again, the same caveat about swim and bike-specific training apply here. You want to be able to perform these workouts without thinking about your form or fit, and that will enable you to focus purely on fitness and speed.

If you find that the workouts here are too advanced for your skill level, it might be more prudent to target a different race a couple of months down the road. However, if that's not possible or preferable, try to focus on each segment of the workout in this plan but tailored to your specific fitness level (your own speed) so you can complete each segment properly and get the benefits of the training structure.

	SWIM	BIKE	RUN
WEEK 1			
MON	**SWIM 1000M** • Warm Up with 400m free form • 1 x 100m free tempo (45 sec rest) • 1 x 200m free tempo (30 sec rest) • 1 x 100m free tempo (45 sec rest) • Warm Down with 100m breaststroke and backstroke easy	OFF	OFF
TUES	DAY OFF		
WED	OFF	**RIDE 60 MINUTES** • 60 min easy ride • **Run off bike:** 10 min easy run	OFF
THURS	OFF		**RUN 30 MINUTES** • 10 min run/walk easy • 10 min tempo run • 10 min run/walk easy
FRI	DAY OFF		
SAT	**SWIM 1200M** • Warm Up with 400m free form • 6 x 100m hard (45 sec rest) • Warm Down with 100m breaststroke and backstroke easy	**RIDE 60 MINUTES** • 20 min easy ride • 15 min tempo ride • 5 min easy ride • 10 min hard ride • 10 min easy ride • **Run off bike:** 10 min easy run	OFF
SUN	OFF		**RUN 35 MINUTES** • 2 min walk • 30 min easy run • 3 min walk

WEEK 2	SWIM	BIKE	RUN
MON	**SWIM 1600M** • Warm Up with 400m free form • 1 x 100m free tempo (30 sec rest) • 1 x 200m free tempo (45 sec rest) • 1 x 400m free tempo (60 sec rest) • 1 x 200m free tempo (45 sec rest) • 1 x 100m free tempo (30 sec rest) • Warm Down with 100m breaststroke and backstroke easy	OFF	OFF
TUES	DAY OFF		
WED	OFF	**RIDE 75 MINUTES** • 20 min easy ride • 25 min tempo ride • 5 min easy ride • 15 min hard ride • 10 min easy ride • **Run off bike:** 10 min easy run	OFF
THURS	OFF		**RUN 35 MINUTES** • 10 min run/walk easy • 15 min tempo run • 10 min run/walk easy
FRI	DAY OFF		
SAT	**SWIM 1400M** • Warm Up with 400m free form • 2 x 50m free hard (20 sec rest) • 6 x 100m free tempo (30 sec rest) • 2 x 50m free hard (20 sec rest) • Warm Down with 100m breaststroke and backstroke easy	**RIDE 75 MINUTES** • 75 min easy ride • **Run off bike:** 10 min easy run	OFF
SUN	OFF		**RUN 40 MINUTES** • 2 min walk • 35 min easy run • 3 min walk

WEEK 3	SWIM	BIKE	RUN
MON	**SWIM 2000M** • Warm Up with 400m free form • 2 x 50m free hard (20 sec rest) • 2 x 100m free tempo (30 sec rest) • 1 x 200m free tempo (45 sec rest) • 1 x 400m free tempo (60 sec rest) • 1 x 200 free tempo (45 sec rest) • 2 x 100m free tempo (30 sec rest) • 2 x 50m free hard (20 sec rest) • Warm Down with 100m breaststroke and backstroke easy	OFF	OFF
TUES	DAY OFF		
WED	OFF	**RIDE 75 MINUTES** • 20 min easy ride • 25 min tempo ride • 5 min easy ride • 15 min hard ride • 10 min easy ride • **Run off bike:** 10 min easy run	OFF
THURS	OFF		**RUN 40 MINUTES** • 6 min run/walk easy • 10 min tempo run • 2 min run/walk easy • 5 min hard run • 2 min run/walk easy • 10 min tempo run • 5 min run/walk easy
FRI	DAY OFF		
SAT	**SWIM 1600M** • Warm Up with 400m free form • 2 x 50m hard (20 sec rest) • 8 x 100m free tempo (30 sec rest) • 2 x 50 m free hard (20 sec rest) • Warm Down with 100m breaststroke and backstroke easy	**60 MINUTE TRANSITION** • 15 min easy ride **Transition Set:** • 10 min hard ride followed by 7 min hard run off the bike. Repeat x 2. • 5 min easy ride	OFF
SUN	OFF		**RUN 45 MINUTES** • 2 min walk • 40 min easy run • 3 min walk

WEEK 4	SWIM	BIKE	RUN
MON	**SWIM 2200M** • Warm Up with 400m free form • 2 x 50m free hard (20 sec rest) • 1 x 100m free tempo (30 sec rest) • 1 x 200m free tempo (45 sec rest) • 1 x 400m free tempo (60 sec rest) • 1 x 200 free tempo (45 sec rest) • 1 x 100m free tempo (30 sec rest) • 2 x 50m free hard (20 sec rest) • Warm Down with 100m breaststroke and backstroke easy	OFF	OFF
TUES		DAY OFF		
WED	OFF	**RIDE 90 MINUTES** • 30 min easy ride • 30 min tempo ride • 5 min easy ride • 15 min hard ride • 10 min easy ride **Run off bike:** 10 min easy run	OFF
THURS		OFF		**RUN 45 MINUTES** • 6 min run/walk easy • 12 min tempo run • 2 min run/walk easy • 5 min hard run • 2 min run/walk easy • 12 min tempo run • 6 min run/walk easy
FRI		DAY OFF		
SAT	**SWIM 1600M** • Warm Up with 100m free form • 200m free as 50 hard 50 easy • Warm Down with 100m breaststroke and backstroke easy	**75 MINUTE TRANSITION** • 20 min easy ride • **Transition Set:** 10 min hard ride followed by 8 run off the bike. Repeat x 2. • 20 min easy ride	OFF
SUN		OFF		**RUN 55 MINUTES** • 2 min walk • 45 min easy run • 3 min walk

WEEK 5	SWIM	BIKE	RUN
MON	**SWIM 22000M** • Warm Up with 400m free form • 2 x 50m free hard (20 sec rest) • 1 x 100m free tempo (30 sec rest) • 1 x 200m free tempo (45 sec rest) • 1 x 400m free tempo (60 sec rest) • 1 x 200m free tempo (45 sec rest) • 2 x 100m free tempo (30 sec rest) • 2 x 50m free hard (20 sec rest) • Warm Down with 100m breaststroke and backstroke easy	OFF	OFF
TUES	DAY OFF		
WED	OFF	**RIDE 75 MINUTES** • 20 min easy ride • 25 min tempo ride • 5 min easy ride • 15 min hard ride • 10 min easy ride • **Run off bike:** 10 min easy run	OFF
THURS	OFF		**RUN 45 MINUTES** • 6 min run/walk easy • 12 min tempo run • 2 min run/walk easy • 5 min hard run • 2 min run/walk easy • 12 min tempo run • 6 min run/walk easy
FRI	DAY OFF		
SAT	**SWIM 1600M** • Warm Up with 400m free form • 2 x 50m free hard (20 sec rest) • 8 x 100m free tempo (30 sec rest) • 2 x 50m free hard (20 sec rest) • Warm Down with 100m breaststroke and backstroke easy	**75 MINUTES TRANSITION** • 20 min easy ride • **Transition Set:** 10 min hard ride followed by 8 run off the bike. Repeat x 2. • 20 min easy run	OFF
SUN	OFF		**RUN 40 MINUTES** • 2 min walk • 35 min easy run • 3 min walk

WEEK 6	SWIM	BIKE	RUN
MON	**SWIM 2200M** • Warm Up with 400m free form • 1 x 100m free tempo (30 sec rest) • 1 x 200m free tempo (45 sec rest) • 1 x 400m free tempo (60 sec rest) • 1 x 200m free tempo (45 sec rest) • 1 x 100m free tempo (30 sec rest) • Warm Down with 100m breaststroke and backstroke easy	OFF	OFF
TUES	\multicolumn{3}{c}{DAY OFF}		
WED	OFF	**RIDE 60 MINUTES** • 20 min easy ride • 15 min tempo ride • 5 min easy ride • 10 min hard ride • 10 min easy ride • **Run off bike:** 10 min easy run	OFF
THURS	\multicolumn{2}{c}{OFF}		**RUN 30 MINUTES** • 6 min run/walk easy • 5 min tempo run • 2 min run/walk easy • 5 min hard run • 2 min run/walk easy • 5 min tempo run • 5 min run/walk easy
FRI	\multicolumn{3}{c}{DAY OFF}		
SAT	**SWIM 400M** • Warm Up with 100m free form • 200m free as 50 hard 50 easy • Warm Down with 100m breaststroke and backstroke easy	**20 MIN – 30 MIN RIDE** • 2-3 x 1 min tempo ride with full recovery between each 1 min tempo	**RUN 5 MIN – 10 MIN OFF BIKE** • 2-3 x 30 sec tempo during run with full recovery between each 30 sec tempo

SUNDAY – Race Day!

General Training Tips for Triathletes

You have probably already heard of these tips but these are important so it's worthwhile to repeat them for emphasis.

1. Schedule your training. Life often gets in the way of being an athlete so the best way to be prepared is to treat your training like it's an important event. Think of it as a meeting that you must attend and allocate a slot for it in your busy schedule. Make sure you plan ahead so you can anticipate potential conflicts and adjust accordingly to ensure that the training plan is followed no matter the situation.

2. Don't cram. If you end up missing one or two sessions, don't try to recover by bundling all sessions together into one. That's the perfect recipe for an injury or over-fatigue and that can have devastating consequences for your condition on race day. Instead of cramming, just leave the sessions you missed and move on to the next one.

3. Be methodical with your training. Track your metrics. Don't leave anything to chance. If you don't track your metrics, you'll have a hard time evaluating your progress. Track your time, distance, heart rate and other important indicators so you can plot them and see your improvement.

4. Find your own routine. Some athletes thrive in doing early morning runs; if you are not that type of person, don't force yourself to be one. Find a routine that works for you and stick with it. You're better off running in the evenings in a good mood than trying to do it during the morning when you're all sleepy and weak.

5. Get some sleep. Sleep is the secret ingredient to successful training. Lack of sleep means poor recovery, bad mood, and

many other unpleasant things. Make sure you get at least 8 hours of sleep every training night.

6. Don't forget about nutrition. This will be the subject of discussion in the next chapter.

Chapter in Summary

Now you have your very own training plans to help you finish a sprint or standard distance race. Just keep an eye on the specific training goals and work towards completing each recommended workout and you'll be powering to the finish line in no time at all.

CHAPTER 6. NUTRITION AND HYDRATION BASICS

We're almost ready to have you racing your first triathlon but we cannot do that without touching on nutrition and hydration. With all the training that you're doing, fueling your body properly is an important component of triathlon success.

Nutrition Tips

In recent years, as our understanding of proper nutrition has broadened, we've come to appreciate the value of healthy carbs as the right fuel for our bodies. Triathlon is no different. We all burn a lot of calories working out and we need to replenish that properly in order to remain effective.

Healthy carbs like brown rice, oatmeal and quinoa should be a main feature of your daily diet. Fruits are also great for providing vitamins and minerals to complete your daily nutrition profile. Lean meats are also great sources of protein and seafood can be a great source of minerals and fatty acids.

At the end of the day, you need to eat the right types of foods in the right quantities and at the right time.

Which brings us to the important nutrition tips that will help you be better prepared for your workouts.

- Before a workout, try to eat about an hour before to allow your body to digest the food. Eat reasonable portions and not big meals or you might just as well say goodbye to your workout. A bowl of cereal, a glass of milk or smoothie, and bread are often enough to get you powered up for a nice session.

- During your training, the nutrition demands vary according to the duration and prevailing conditions wherever it is that you're training. Shorter workouts like bike rides or runs can be managed with sports bars and energy gels. You can even make your own granola bar at home and use that on extended bike and run sessions. There's no general rule that applies to everyone as to when to eat during a ride or run but 40-45 per gel or bar is a good start. Over time, try to pay attention to your own needs and pick a strategy that works for you.

- Post-workout, try to eat within 30 minutes so you can quickly get nutrients into your body to initiate recovery. Healthy carbs remain the main feature here but hydrating properly, as will be tackled in the next section, is also important.

- Overall diet. It's hard to give a hard and fast rule on triathlon diets because we all have different needs. Start with a 60-20-20 carb-to-fat-to-protein ratio and adjust accordingly from there. You can use your weight and body fat percentage to see how your diet interacts with your training. The main goal is to maintain (or even lose) weight but you should also look into lowering your body fat percentage. A rigorous training plan with a healthy diet will get you in proper shape for race day.

Hydration Basics

Water is your body's best friend but we all know it is not enough. When you sweat, you lose electrolytes and failure to replace these can lead to all sorts of problems starting with cramps.

To prevent this, hydrate with sports drinks or hydration options with electrolytes. Gatorade is a common example and this works for many but there are also more options that have come to the market in recent years. You should try to find which one works for you. Some people like carbonated sports drinks while others hate it and you can never really tell which side of the camp you belong until you try it.

When in training, try to drink 5-8 ounces of liquid every 15 minutes. You'll need more if you're in hot weather so plan ahead and try to anticipate your re-fueling pit stops if you are out riding or running. Don't get caught without a hydration plan because that can have devastating consequences to your training or race.

It's also important to try to optimize your hydration by not over-doing it. Excessive water intake can lead to a condition known as hypernatremia where the body loses a lot of electrolytes and the concentration in your body falls below an acceptable threshold. Hypernatremia can be fatal much like dehydration so you should keep an eye on this to minimize the risk of it happening to you.

One additional thing to note: if you are up for long rides or runs, you might want to consider getting equipment that can help you stay hydrated at all times. For the bike, you'll have water bottles filled with your chosen sports drink while on the run, you can always opt for hydration belts. It's important that you are aware of these options so you can systematically plan your training and even race hydration needs accordingly.

Chapter in Summary

Nutrition and hydration in triathlon is very important but it is not complicated. The trick is to get your needs dialed down in training and to simply adapt them on race day. When you train, pay attention to what you eat and drink and how your body responds to these. If necessary, adjust accordingly.

If you do this properly in training, there should be no reason that you can't eat and hydrate properly on race day.

CHAPTER 7. RACE DAY

All your hard work has been leading to this! It's race day. This is it.

Now what?

Good question. It's easy to get caught up in the excitement that you'll end up missing a few things if you're not methodical with your approach. Here are some race day tips you should keep in mind to be in total control of your preparations for the big day.

1. **Arrive early.** You've read this before, you'll read it again: there is no substitute for prudence and planning. It does not matter a lot if you are prepared but you arrive late and you end up hurrying yourself.

   To avoid this, arrive early. You'll have to go through the motions of parking your car, checking into transition, getting your body marking, fitting in all the stickers and marking, and setting up your transition area. You also need to spend some time getting familiar with the transition area layout, your bike location relative to the entrance and exits, and your route to get to your bike and out. You can't do these if you don't have enough time.

   Save yourself the trouble and arrive early so there's plenty of time to do all that needs to be done.

2. **Be meticulous with your preparations.** Go through your checklist the day before and pack your stuff properly. Below is a sample checklist that you can modify according to your specific requirements.

GENERAL
- ☐ Watch or heart rate monitor & band
- ☐ Energy bars, gels & fluids
- ☐ Sunscreen
- ☐ Talcum powder (for shoes)
- ☐ Vaseline (to prevent chaffing)
- ☐ Race belt (if wearing a race number)
- ☐ Race kit (swim cap, stickers, wrist & timing band)
- ☐ Spare pair of shoes – remember you will learn your race ones in transition

SWIM
- ☐ Swim suit or tri suit
- ☐ Wetsuit
- ☐ Plastic bags (to help put wetsuit on)
- ☐ Goggles x 2 (or spare strap/nose piece)
- ☐ Ear and nose plugs if required
- ☐ Swim cap (part of your race kit)
- ☐ Body Glide, baby oil or Vaseline (to help remove wetsuit)
- ☐ Transition towel (brightly coloured)

BIKE
- ☐ Bike and helmet (Entry will be refused if not of an appropriate standard)
- ☐ Bike shoes or runners
- ☐ Socks (if required)
- ☐ Sunglasses
- ☐ Track pump (or check tyre pressure beforehand)
- ☐ Tool bag with spare tubes and repair tools
- ☐ Water bottles x 2
- ☐ Race wheels (if you are a speed demon!)
- ☐ Electrical tape (to fasten gels or repair kit to your bike)
- ☐ Bike computer

RUN
- ☐ Running shoes with elastic laces
- ☐ Socks (if required)
- ☐ Hat (to keep sun off and to keep wet/cool)
- ☐ Sunglasses (second clean pair if required)

POST RACE
- ☐ Clothing (dry, warm clothing for post race recovery)
- ☐ Recovery nutrition

If you need to, lay all your stuff on the bed and pack each item carefully so you don't forget anything. Make sure you have your nutrition and hydration plan ready and accounted for. (I had a friend who packed a bag of energy gels for a race but left them inside his car during the race.)

The same goes for your bike. Have it checked and tuned-up days before to make sure all potential problems are foreseen and addressed.

3. **Don't try anything new on race day.** Go with the tri suit you've been using for training. Don't experiment with new nutrition and hydration options. Stick with what has worked and you won't have to deal with as many unexpected things when you race.

4. **Be conservative with your race pace.** It's easy to get carried away in the heat of the moment and you end up swimming or biking or running too fast out of the gate. That's a perfect recipe for bonking or running out of fuel before the finish and you wouldn't want that to happen to you.

   You've trained for a specific race pace but be attentive to your body and listen accordingly. There will be more races in the future for you to set a good time. If you don't feel great on race day, adjust accordingly and pace yourself sufficiently so you can finish strong.

5. **Have fun!** That's the simplest and most powerful advice you can ever receive. You are now living your triathlon dream so enjoy the moment and just have fun!

Congratulations on completing your triathlon journey!

May you be motivated to do more in the future, for health or whatever it is that drives you to train and race a triathlon. It won't be easy, for sure, but if you pay attention to the lessons in training and the ideas we talked about here, there is little doubt that you are in for a bright future in triathlon racing!

Kudos, and see you at the finish line!

CONCLUSION

Completing your first triathlon is an extraordinary achievement. It wouldn't have happened if not for countless training miles in the water, on your bike, and during the run.

We hope that the training tips we've shared are instrumental towards making you finally realize your triathlon dream. We also hope that this will be the first of many more races for you. We also encourage you to share your story and inspire others to take up the triathlon challenge just as you did. It might be daunting at first but you know it is doable and it's time to have others share in the joy of triathlon racing.

We thank you for trusting us with your triathlon journey and we hope to see you in future races wherever you may be in the world!

All the Best

Richard

ABOUT THE AUTHOR

Richard has been interested in Sport and Exercise for most of my life. He grew up trying many different sports, and rarely keeping to one. As soon as he felt he had improved in one area, he would look out for the next challenge.

This process continued with exercise as he transitioned into an adult life. He's always been curious about challenging himself and seeing what he's capable of. This inquisitive nature led to him trying many new activities and entering a variety of competitions. Richard has completed Half Marathons, Marathons, Ultra Marathons, Obstacle Courses, Off Road, and Mountain Races. Not content with running, he went on to complete Triathlons, Duathlons, 5km Open Water Swims and 100km Bike races. His numerous cardiovascular escapades has resulted in him having a resting heart rate of 36 beats per minute.

More recently, Richard switched his focus onto strength training and experimented with various types of weight training, gymnastics, and functional strength. Predictably, the new trials were quickly followed by him entering competitions in the chosen activity. He's since entered Powerlifting,

Bodybuilding and Olympic Weightlifting events.

A life changing moment happened for him when he was first exposed to Crossfit (Functional Fitness). Finally, he had found an activity that warranted all-around physical ability. You had to be fit, fast, flexible, strong, co-ordinated, powerful, and skilful. This sport was made for him! He now follows a Crossfit style training approach to this day.

OTHER BOOKS BY RICHARD BOND

Your First Marathon

A Beginners Guide To Marathon Training, Marathon Preparation And Completing Your First Marathon

Mental Toughness

A Guide to Developing Peak Performance and an Unbeatable Mind in Everyday Life

Fitbit

The Complete Guide To Using Fitbit For Weight Loss and Increased Performance

Garmin Vivoactive

The Complete Guide to Using the Garmin Vivoactive

Printed in Great Britain
by Amazon